Series Editor: Catherine Bowness

The **Faith in Action** Series

A Life for a Life?

The Story of Helen Prejean

Deborah Helme

Illustrated by Brian Platt

RELIGIOUS AND MORAL EDUCATION PRESS

A LIFE FOR A LIFE?

The Story of Helen Prejean

Click, click, click – then silence. When the switch was turned it clicked loudly. At the first click nineteen hundred volts were released. The second click released only five hundred. On the third click another nineteen hundred volts went racing through the wires. This final click seemed to echo around the room.

Sister Helen Prejean had bowed her head and closed her eyes tightly. She could still hear the clicking in her head but realized everyone around her was totally quiet and still. She prayed for God's help and slowly opened her eyes. She looked through the window in front of her into the room next door. There was a man sitting in a large wooden chair. Thick leather straps tied him to it firmly. He had a metal cap on his head and his face was covered with a grey cloth. His left hand gripped the arm of the chair, but the fingers on his right hand curled upwards. He was totally still. He was dead.

Half an hour later, Helen walked towards the high prison wall. It was one o'clock in the morning, but there were crowds of people waiting outside the prison gates. As soon as Helen passed the final armed guard into freedom she was dazzled by cameras flashing. The American press rushed forward to get their questions answered first. Despite the noise and the shouting, she managed to hear some of the questions:

'Miss Prejean, why do you help murderers?'

'Do you think he's going to hell?'

'Who are the victims?'

'Don't you know the Bible says, "an eye for an eye, a tooth for a tooth"? How can anyone forgive a killer?'

She said nothing and slowly walked through the disappointed media.

'I can't believe she looks so ordinary,' commented one of the journalists.

By the time she reached her car, parked just a short distance from the gates, Helen was shaking so much she could hardly open the door. As she sank into the driver's seat, she knew she was too upset to drive home. She leant her head on the steering-wheel and through her tears she tried to make sense of what had happened that night. The face of a young man flashed in her mind, a young man with sharp piercing eyes and a pointed jaw line. Just hours earlier she had watched him eat his last meal, then say his last prayer and take his last breath.

She already knew that witnessing an execution that night would change her life. 'Please give me strength, Lord God,' she prayed. 'What am I doing here? I'm a nun. How did I get involved in this? What am I going to do now?'

What Do You Think?

Important: In answering 'What Do You Think?' questions in this book, it is important that you not only state your opinion but also give as many reasons as possible for your opinion.

1. What do you think 'an eye for an eye and a tooth for a tooth' means?

2. Is it ever possible to forgive someone who has committed murder?

3. The Ten Commandments state, 'You must not kill.' Should this include not using capital punishment (the death penalty)?

David and Loretta

One evening, seventeen-year-old David LeBlanc and his girlfriend Loretta Bourque set off to watch a football match at their local high school. It probably seemed just an ordinary day in an ordinary week, but what happened that night was to shatter their families' happiness for ever.

David and Loretta never came home that evening. Perhaps their parents waited up until after midnight for them to come in, or maybe they went to bed and lay awake for ages hoping to hear the key in the door, before falling into an uneasy sleep.

The following day was Saturday, so it could have been midmorning before anyone checked David and Loretta's rooms and found their beds hadn't been slept in. Their parents may have phoned the couple's friends one by one to see if anyone knew where they were. Then perhaps they tried to remain calm and rang local hospitals to see if there had been some kind of accident. At some stage someone must have contacted the police. Then there was nothing more the two families could do – just wait and hope.

Two days later Lloyd LeBlanc, David's father, was asked to accompany the police to identify the body of a young man. He saw his son lying in a field next to Loretta. They had both been shot in the head. Lloyd knelt down by his son and prayed.

Later two men were arrested for the apparently mindless murder of the two teenagers.

What Do You Think?

1. Why do parents often wait up for their teenage children?

2. How do you feel when you are given restrictions on the time you are allowed out or the places you are allowed to go? If you were a parent why do you think you might put restrictions on your child?

3. What kinds of emotions do you think Lloyd LeBlanc would have felt when he saw his son? What might he have felt about the murderers?

Helen Writes to a Prisoner

In June 1981, Helen packed all her personal belongings into a small, brown van and set off for her new home in the St Thomas Housing Project. She had been safe and comfortable all her life. She had come from a wealthy family and as a young woman had chosen to become a nun. She had enjoyed devoting much of her life to prayer. Now she was in her forties and suddenly her life was going to be very different. Her new address, '519 St Andrew Street, St Thomas, New Orleans', sounded perfect for a nun, however it was an area famous for its guns, crime and disease. The St Thomas Housing Project was home to fifteen hundred very poor people. 'At least, I'm not here on my own,' thought Helen, as she stared up at the flat and began to unpack the van. As she started to move all the boxes she was glad she no longer had to wear a habit, sometimes that traditional dress was so impractical. She was joining four other nuns who had also decided to live there to try to bring Christian hope to people who often felt hopeless.

The next day she wrote in her diary:

> Didn't sleep much. Noisy until about 3 a.m. People standing on the corner talking and drinking. Feel nervous, unsettled. Heard a gunshot. Had checked when I got into bed to make sure my bed was under the windowsill in case a bullet came through. Is this New Orleans? I feel like I'm in another country.

All around her, Helen found people who were struggling with unemployment, family break-ups, debt, drug addiction, homelessness and violence. Together with the other nuns and their co-workers she tried to find ways to help. She taught basic maths and English in an adult education centre. She advised people who didn't know how to pay their bills. She helped people to write letters to housing departments and the social security. There was always plenty to do.

One day, about six months after the move, she had just finished teaching an English class when one of her colleagues called by to see her. He worked for a charity that helped to support prisoners. He asked her if she would consider becoming a pen friend to a prisoner on Death Row. Helen paused for a moment and said, 'OK'. She had no idea then that the decision would change her life.

Later that evening she looked at the name she had been given: 'Elmo Patrick Sonnier, number 95281, Death Row, Angola'. Helen had been told that Sonnier had been involved in the terrible murder of two teenagers. David LeBlanc and Loretta Bourque had been on their way home from watching a school football match. Patrick Sonnier and his brother Eddie were high on drugs when they had dragged the young people out of the car, raped Loretta and shot them both in the head at close range.

Hearing about the details of the crime made Helen feel sick and angry. She knew Sonnier had done wrong and she believed that he should be punished. She looked down in horror at the name. Did she really want to write to a man who had done something like that? She thought for a few moments. This man had done a terrible, wicked thing, but he was still a human being. Slowly she began to write a letter, explaining who she was and telling him a little about herself and her job. She told him he didn't have to write back, she would carry on writing to him anyway. She shivered as she wrote 'Death Row' on the envelope.

Several weeks later she received a letter from Sonnier, who said he would like to write to her. He explained how he'd tried 'going it alone'. He knew he was going to die, so he had decided not to get to know anyone new. But he admitted he found this hard, so now he'd like to write to someone. When the guard threw a letter on to the floor of his cell, he thought it must be a mistake. No one would want to write to him.

Helen wrote back and began to receive letters from Sonnier regularly. In them he described his life on Death Row. His own cell was 2 metres wide and 2½ metres long. He had to spend twenty-three hours of every day in this space. Sometimes he was allowed to visit other inmates on the Row but he preferred to keep himself to himself. He wrote about all sorts of things, but never mentioned his crime or his future death. After they had been writing for a few months, Sonnier sent a photo of himself. It had been taken after his arrest. Looking at the photo was the first time Helen had seen his face. There was something about his expression that made her feel nervous. She felt safer knowing he was in prison.

Helen knew he never had any visitors. She tried to imagine how she would feel, not talking to anyone day after day, with nothing to look forward to and no one coming to visit her. Finally, after a lot of thought, she applied for permission to visit Sonnier.

What Do You Think?

1. Why you think Sister Helen chose to live in the St Thomas area? How do you think she felt when her life changed so much? How do you cope with new situations?

2. Why do you think some of the people who lived in the St Thomas area felt hopeless? The house that the nuns lived in became called 'Hope House'. What does this tell you about their work? Would they have been able to offer struggling people as much help if they had continued to live in their convent?

3. A chaplain is a church minister or other religious leader who works in an institution like a hospital, a school or a prison. Why do you think prisons have chaplains? What might a prison chaplain be asked to do?

4. What religious reasons might someone give for working with prisoners?

5. Imagine you are an adult who has been asked to write to a prisoner convicted of a serious crime. How might you react and why?

Visiting Death Row

Months later Helen drove out of New Orleans and turned onto Highway 66. She drove past a big blue lake and through dark, leafy green hills. It made a refreshing change to be away from the heat, noise and smell of the city. Yet Helen could not relax and enjoy the journey as the road lead to Angola Prison. She was going to meet a murderer.

By European standards, Angola was a huge prison, with over four and a half thousand prisoners. Helen shuddered as she drove to the front gate and saw several armed guards. They thoroughly searched her car before letting her into the prison grounds. She went through several more security checks before she was escorted to Death Row. As she walked to the entrance she was surprised to pass a small pond with ducks on it and see lots of flowers near the path. 'It's just like a quiet little park,' she thought.

Inside the building a guard led her down a corridor divided up by a series of gates. Each gate clanged shut after them. The sound of metal on metal echoed everywhere. It was also very, very hot. Eventually she was shown into the visiting-room. Despite the intense heat Helen was so nervous she felt cold. There was no one else in the room, so she walked up and down trying to take deep breaths to feel calm. Finally she heard muffled voices approaching and the sound of metal scraping the concrete. With a shudder, Helen realized that Sonnier must be walking with his feet were chained together. When she saw him, she noticed his hands were chained too.

Surprisingly he seemed relaxed and friendly. 'Am I glad to see you, Sister,' he said grinning at her. He looked different from the photo. Helen had been told her visit could last a maximum of two hours and she had thought what a long time that would be. But time passed quickly as Sonnier told her about his childhood, his family and his life. He told her about his life in the prison. He described his tiny cell and how he kept all his belongings in a small box under his bed and used it for weight-lifting. He told her about the other eleven men in his section of Death Row and how they found it hard to get along and often threw things at each other through the bars. Helen realized all she had to do was listen as Sonnier was simply grateful for the opportunity to talk. Despite the ordeal of that first visit, Helen continued to visit him on Death Row every month. He found it easy to talk to her, but he never mentioned his crime.

When Helen had applied for permission to visit Sonnier she was described as his spiritual adviser. Each Death Row inmate was allowed a spiritual adviser of their choice. This person was responsible for the spiritual well-being of the prisoner, particularly in the final days and hours of their life. Helen took this role very seriously. She wanted to help Sonnier prepare for his death, and to think about life after death. She believed he would have to face God for his final judgement. She thought it was important that he took responsibility for his crimes and was sorry for them.

Eventually he began to talk about his crimes when she asked him if he felt God had forgiven him for the murders. Sonnier had paused for a while and then said,

'At first I felt that even God hated me, but now I have a lot of time to read the Bible. My favourite part is Psalm 31, sometimes I think it was written just for me.'

All my enemies, and especially my neighbours,
treat me with contempt;
those who know me are afraid of me;
when they see me in the street, they run away.
Everyone has forgotten me, as though I were dead;
I am like something thrown away.
I hear many enemies whispering;
terror is all around me.
They are making plans against me, plotting to kill me.
But my trust is in you, O Lord,
You are my God.

(Psalm 31)

'I am sorry for what I have done. I don't think people can forgive me, but I think God can,' he told her thoughtfully.

Helen was thankful that they were finally talking about such important things. In her letters and on her visits, she started suggesting different parts of the Bible that he could read which she thought would help him. She told him she was praying for him.

What Do You Think?

1. Why do you think first impressions are often so important? How do you judge people when you meet them? What kind of impression do you think you give people? How do you feel about being labelled?

2. Helen had to pass through several security checks before entering Death Row. What surprised her after she had passed them?

3. Why did Helen think it was important to try to prepare Sonnier for his death?

4. Christians and Muslims believe they will be judged by God when they die. What do you think happens when someone dies?

5. Sonnier believed that God might forgive him. Why did Sonnier believe this?

An Eye for an Eye, a Tooth for a Tooth

Sometime in July 1983, about eighteen months after Helen had written that first letter, she was surprised to receive a phone call from Sonnier. His voice sounded strained and he struggled to keep talking, 'They've given me a date, my date.' Helen froze as she realized he was talking about an execution date. That morning a guard had stopped in front of his cell and handed him a piece of paper to read and sign. It said: 'Warrant of Execution in Capital Case, Elmo Patrick Sonnier, the condemned person to be put to death, the 19th day of August 1983'.

Helen started to visit him every week and was shocked by his appearance. He looked thin and almost yellow. He had dark circles under his eyes. Every time he tried to eat he was sick and had lost over two stone in two weeks. He kept going on coffee and cigarettes. Each time Helen visited she found herself calculating how many more days he had to live, how many more Mondays, Tuesdays, Wednesdays, Thursdays.

Two days before his execution date she was allowed to make a four-hour visit. She talked and talked, asking him questions and telling him stories, trying to calm him down. Every now and then he tried to laugh, but his laugh sounded false and there was still terror in his eyes. As she drove away after the visit, she turned on the radio. She heard on the news that his execution had been postponed until further court appeals had been completed.

Helen found it hard to believe that the State was really going to kill Sonnier in cold blood. At the same time she was haunted by the thought of his young victims, David and Loretta. She felt guilty for befriending their killer. She thought about their parents' suffering. Sonnier had condemned Mr and Mrs LeBlanc and Mr and Mrs Bourque to a life sentence of pain. They would always wonder what David and Loretta's last few hours had been like. For the rest of their lives they would fear for their other children. They would

have nightmares. They had suffered from a horror that would never leave them. Perhaps people who had suffered like them had every right to call for 'an eye for an eye, a tooth for a tooth, a life for a life'?

This phrase comes from the Bible (Exodus 21:23–24). Helen had often heard it quoted by people who were in favour of the death penalty. Yet it was also possible to use parts of the Bible to argue against the death penalty. For example, Jesus had encouraged his followers to forgive their enemies instead of responding to hate with hate or violence with violence:

> You have heard that it was said, 'An eye for an eye, and a tooth for a tooth.' But now I tell you: do not take revenge on someone who wrongs you. If anyone slaps you on the right cheek, let him slap your left cheek too.
>
> (Matthew 5:38–39)

Since she had been writing to Sonnier, Helen had become familiar with many of the arguments for and against capital punishment. People in favour of the death penalty said that execution was a deterrent: that is, a warning to others not to commit similar crimes. They also said that execution prevented the murderer from ever being able to kill anyone else.

For each argument for capital punishment, Helen had heard arguments against. Despite extensive research there was no conclusive proof to suggest that in areas where capital punishment was enforced there were fewer violent murders. Some argued that it made society more brutal, giving out the message that it was all right to counter violence with more violence. Another concern was that if someone was executed and later evidence proved they had been innocent there was no way to reverse the punishment. If executions were acceptable for certain crimes, were they acceptable for everyone who was convicted of those crimes? For example, should children or people with learning difficulties ever face the death penalty? What right did human beings ever have to decide if someone should live or die?

What Do You Think?

1. Some countries have abolished the death penalty. Why do you think they have done this? Why do you think other places have retained the death penalty?

2. 'Now I know he is dead, I feel that I can live again. Justice has been done. At last I know he has suffered like my daughter suffered. We, the victims, should be able to decide what happens to the murderers.' These are the words of a man who watched the murderer of his daughter being executed. Do you think relatives of people who have been murdered should be able to decide what happens to the killer? Give reasons for your answer.

3. Helen said, 'If I were killed, I know I wouldn't want my murderers to be executed.' Why do you think she said this?

4. When an eight-year-old boy heard that Sonnier had been killed because he had killed someone, he asked: 'Who is going to kill the man who killed Sonnier?' What would you say to the boy?

5. Why do Christians have different views about capital punishment?

Waiting to Die

Months later the court appeals failed and Sonnier received yet another date for execution, this time for 4 April 1984. This was his third date and everyone knew there was little hope of it being postponed again. He returned to living on a diet of cigarettes and coffee. He tried to stay awake at night as he suffered from terrible nightmares.

Several days before the execution he was moved from Death Row to the 'Death House'. This was a small, specially designed one-storey building. It was in the centre of the huge prison complex. It looked like an ordinary prison building, except that there were several armed guards outside. Along the front wall there were four big tubs of bright-red flowers. Inside there was a large entrance area, several offices, a visiting-room, four small concrete cells, and the execution chamber – the room with the electric chair. On one of the walls in this room there was a big glass window allowing witnesses to sit in the room next door and watch the execution.

It was usual for prisoners to be moved into the Death House a few days before they were due to be executed. They were never told when they would go and were often taken in the middle of the night, so they would not disturb the other prisoners. Once in the Death House, they would never come out alive. The prison authorities knew that prisoners would be desperate to escape or even take their own life themselves, so they were under constant guard.

As Helen was Sonnier's spiritual adviser, she was able to visit him in the Death House. As she entered the building for the first time, she felt physically sick, knowing that she was so close to the place where Sonnier was going to be killed. As she approached his cell, she was surprised to see him watching basketball on television. The guard on duty had moved nearer to the cell to watch the game too. Suddenly one team scored and they both cheered. For one brief moment they were two ordinary men watching sport together. But in a few days' time other guards would be leading Sonnier out of this corridor to his death.

Whenever she had an opportunity Helen asked the prison staff about their work. All the guards were strongly advised not to get to know the prisoners and to look upon them all as con men. This was particularly important for anyone working with those prisoners condemned to death. Helen also spoke to the warden who arranged the details of the execution and the medical staff who oversaw the execution. Everyone explained that it was simply their job, they were carrying out their orders and were following the decision of the courts and the law of the State. No one would accept responsibility for the killing and yet Helen sensed that many of the prison staff suffered from the strain of being so involved.

Sonnier tried to greet Helen cheerfully. He smoked constantly and as his hands were still chained together at his waist this meant that much of the time he was bent double. He looked ill and very very frightened. Helen couldn't believe that she was supposed to be comforting and helping a man who knew he had only a few more days to live. She felt very unqualified for this and yet she knew she was his only hope. She encouraged him to talk as much as possible, about the good and the bad in his life.

'Time's going too quickly,' Sonnier kept saying, as he glanced at the clock. The pressure on him in the Death House seemed unbearable and yet he wanted each moment to last for ever. Suddenly, Helen was told to stand clear of the door and several guards came and led him away. No one explained what was happening, but one of the guards told Helen that Sonnier would be back in about an hour and suggested she waited for him outside in the fresh air. Sonnier had been taken away to be measured and weighed. The guards wanted to make sure they would be able to control him if he became violent on the way to the electric chair the following day.

He arrived back in time for the prayer service Helen had arranged. One of the chaplains in the prison had agreed to join them and the three sat as near to each other as the bars of the cell would allow. It was a simple service. Helen prayed, read from the Bible and together they listened to a hymn. After the service, Sonnier's mood seemed a little lighter. When it was time for Helen to go, he made her promise to get plenty of rest. They both knew that the next day – the last of Sonnier's life – would be a long day. Sonnier was due to be executed just after midnight.

What Do You Think?

1. Why was Helen surprised to see Sonnier and a guard watching basketball on television?

2. Why were the guards advised to think of prisoners as con men and told not to get to know them?

3. The pressure on Sonnier in the Death House seemed unbearable. Some people might say this suffering was part of his punishment. Give reasons for and against this view.

Counting the Hours

Helen didn't sleep well that night. She didn't know how she would get through the next twenty-four hours and kept praying that God would help her. She was comforted to know that many of her family, her friends and her fellow nuns were also praying for her.

Helen arrived at the prison the following day about noon. Before she went to see Sonnier, she first went to see his brother, Eddie. He was an inmate at Angola too, but he had been sentenced to life imprisonment. He was finding the strain of knowing his brother was going to be executed very difficult to cope with. Helen told him how strong Sonnier was and that she would stay with him until the end. She told Eddie she would pray for him and his brother to help them get through the day. When she saw Sonnier she told him about her visit to Eddie.

> 'I'm angry at him,' he said. 'I'm angry at the kids for being parked out in the woods in the first place. I'm angry that Mr Bourque and Mr LeBlanc are coming to watch me die. I'm angry at myself for letting me and Eddie mess with the kids. I'll have a chance to say my last words, and I'm going to tell Bourque and LeBlanc a thing or two, coming to watch me die. Especially Bourque. I've been hearing that he's been telling people he wishes he could pull the switch himself.'

Helen paused for a minute and then quietly said, 'It's your choice if you want your last words to be words of hate. I can understand you wanting to attack people who have come to watch you suffer and die. But I am sure there is a part of you that wants to die a free and loving man. Think about how the parents of the teenagers you killed have suffered. I'm not saying it's easy to make your last words words of kindness, but it's possible and it's up to you.'

In those final hours before the execution it seemed to Helen that time stood still and at the same time it raced by. Somehow, above all the different noises in the Death House she could still hear the clock ticking. Even this close to the execution there was still a small chance that there would be a stay of execution, either from one of the appeal courts or from the Governor of the State. Each time the phone rang, Helen watched nervously to see if it was good news. But each time the warden on duty just shook his head.

Unlike the previous few days, there were a lot of people coming and going. Men in uniform, men in suits. Sonnier watched them all intently as they came and went, often explaining to Helen who they were. 'He's come to check the chair is working,' he said, and, 'That's the head of the goon squad.' 'The goon squad' was the way the prisoners described the men who took the prisoner from the cell and strapped him to the chair.

At 6 p.m. it was time for Sonnier's final meal. He had taken his time over choosing what to order and had finally settled on a steak, medium well done, potato salad, green beans, hot rolls with butter, a green salad, a coke and apple pie for dessert. Somehow, after days of eating nothing, Sonnier managed to eat it all. 'The steak was perfect – tell the chef he did a great job,' he said.

Helen decided to give Sonnier a few minutes to himself and, needing to escape from the horror all around her, locked herself in the ladies' toilet. Desperately she prayed that God would help her carry on and give her the strength she needed to help Sonnier in his final hours. As she slowly walked back to the cell, she noticed how clean and white everything was. The white tiled walls sparkled, there was a white table-cloth on the table in the entrance area, the smell of coffee percolating filled the whole building. In one of the offices there was the sound of someone typing. 'It's like being in a hospital,' Helen thought with a shock, 'but there everyone is trying to save life.'

When Helen returned to the cell, Sonnier was talking on the telephone. It was his lawyer explaining that the Governor had refused his appeal. 'He was my last hope,' said Sonnier, 'I'm going to die.' Immediately Helen started to pray, asking God to comfort him and give him the courage to die with love, not hate in his heart. She felt the prayer pouring out of her, as though God was helping her find the words.

Sometime after 9 p.m. the guards came to shave Sonnier's head, so that his hair couldn't catch fire when he was electrocuted. Helen waited in the entrance area. When she returned to the cell she was shocked to see his grey shiny head. Even his eyebrows had been shaved off.

At 10.30, with just one and a half hours left to live, Sonnier called out to the guard for a pen. In his Bible there was a section for family history - births, marriages and deaths. Slowly, with his hand shaking a little, he filled in the date of his death - 4 April 1984. Then he closed the Bible and handed it to Sister Helen. 'Here you are, Sister,' he said, 'I want you to have this. Thank you for caring for me.'

Finally the guards arrived to take him to the chair. As they came out of the cell one of the guards shouted, 'Dead man walking.' Helen was allowed to touch Sonnier's shoulder and walk with them. She was still holding his Bible and read these words from Isaiah 43:

> Do not be afraid ...
> I have called you by name
> – you are mine.
> When you pass through
> deep waters,
> I will be with you ...
> When you pass through fire
> – you will not be burnt ...

What Do You Think?

1. What did Helen do to try to help Sonnier in the final days of his life?

2. Sonnier found reading the Bible very comforting as he faced death. Read through the first verses of Isaiah 43. Why do you think Helen chose them to read to Sonnier as he walked to the execution chamber? Can you think of any other situations when these words might comfort someone? If you had to choose something to read to a person about to die, what would you choose to read and why?

Watching a Man Die

Finally they reached the execution chamber and said goodbye. Helen went to sit with the witnesses as she had promised, so that Sonnier would see a face that cared about him immediately before he died.

Before he sat in the chair, Sonnier had the chance to say some last words. He had listened to Helen and simply said to the witnesses through the window, 'Mr LeBlanc, I don't want to die hating you. Please will you forgive Eddie and me?'

Then he was strapped to the chair and ten minutes later he was dead.

What Do You Think?

1. Why did Helen witness the execution?

2. Read what Sonnier said about feeling angry (page 13). Suggest why he addressed his last words to Mr LeBlanc only.

3. If you were going to be remembered by the last words you said, what would you want to say?

4. Do you think everyone is afraid of dying? Give reasons.

How Can Anyone Forgive a Killer?

Helen took a deep breath and pushed open the door: another day and another ordeal. The memory and the strain of the execution were beginning to fade. In the days after the execution she had been criticized in the media and had really appreciated the help and support of her friends, family and her fellow nuns during that hard time. She wished things could return to normal, but somehow her experience as a spiritual adviser on Death Row had changed everything and she knew there was no way back.

This was another example of those changes. She quietly slipped into the room and sat down in the circle of people who had already arrived. Gradually the room filled up and people started to talk of their different experiences. Helen was at a self-help group for victims of violent crime.

Someone asked me how many children I had. I didn't know what to say. Am I the mother of five or three? ... two of my boys have been shot ...

My eighty-year-old mother was shot. I think it was because she witnessed a robbery.

I keep thinking I can hear her key in the lock ...

I really dread Christmas and birthdays, they should be happy times, but for me they are sad. They remind me of all that I have lost. Three of my children have died, one died of cot death, then my three-year-old died of meningitis and now my twenty-four-year-old son has been shot.

When Helen had talked to Sonnier about his crime she had often thought about the families of the young couple and wondered how they coped. She had thought about getting in touch but decided that as she had befriended the murderer they would probably want nothing to do with her. She finally met them days before his death at the Pardon Hearing, one of the last opportunities a prisoner has to appeal against the death sentence.

The meeting had been held in a big room, divided down the middle by an aisle. On the left all the seats were blue. These were for anyone on the State's side, like the parents of the two young people murdered, who wanted the execution. On the right the chairs were red. These were for anyone on the side of the prisoner. Helen had been on a red chair and Mr and Mrs LeBlanc and Mr and Mrs Bourque had been on blue chairs. The gap between them could not have been more striking.

During a break in the meeting Helen had introduced herself to Mr and Mrs LeBlanc and Mr and Mrs Bourque. They were very angry with her. They wanted to know what a nun, someone representing the Church, was doing sitting on the side of the criminal. They felt that the Church hadn't come to help and support them. Helen immediately realized she had made a big mistake. She realized she should have contacted the grieving families and offered to try to support them too. She felt uncomfortable and miserable as she thought about how she had let them down. Later, although she thought it was too late, she visited the families of both victims. Lloyd LeBlanc, whose son David had been killed by the Sonnier brothers, gradually overcame his anger and began to explain to her how hard things had been.

He suggested that she would understand the victims' point of view better if she went to one of these meetings for victims of violence. Helen thought she had prepared herself but she was shocked at the way people suffered. She discovered that people had to keep repeating the details of the crime when they heard about it in order to take it in. When someone in a family has been murdered it can take as long as eight months for the rage to wear off and for the reality to sink in. When a child is murdered, the parents often deal with their pain in different ways. On average 70% of these couples will divorce. After a murder people often feel isolated because friends and families avoid them as they don't know what to say. There are certain times in the year when it is particularly hard to cope, like birthdays, Christmas and special family events, when the memories, grief and rage all come back again.

Through listening to story after story of pain and hurt Helen realized that there are no easy answers to forgiving someone. People cannot be forced or hurried into forgiveness. In fact some of the families found that it helped to campaign for the death penalty, as this gave them something to focus on and was a way of getting justice for the person they loved.

What Do You Think?

1. Do you think Helen was wrong not to contact the victims' families when she started visiting Sonnier? Give reasons.

2. People react very differently when someone they love is murdered. Should they try to forgive? Some people might say that forgiving the criminal would mean they were letting the victim down. Do you agree? Give reasons.

Trying to Forgive

After the meeting Lloyd LeBlanc told Helen more about his life after his son had died. For a year after the murder, Lloyd had to take his wife to the grave very frequently – it was almost as if she couldn't go on with daily life until she had been there. He said she cried for about three years. He found it hard to go home as it felt like a tomb there, so he would work long hours to stay away. At the Pardon Hearing, where he had first met Helen, he had represented the families in asking for the execution to be carried out, but now this troubled him. His future seemed empty.

As the years passed after the execution, Helen kept in touch with Lloyd LeBlanc. One day he explained to her that praying was very important to him. He prayed about everything. He prayed for his wife and he prayed in thanksgiving for his daughter and her four young children who helped his wife live again. He even prayed for the Sonnier family. He thought a lot about Patrick and Eddie's mother: she had lost two sons – one was dead and the other was in prison for life. When he heard that she was ill and dying, he visited her to try to comfort her in some way. He even gave Helen money to help her prison visiting though he knew that one of the people she visited was Eddie Sonnier, one of the brothers who had killed his son.

Lloyd LeBlanc told Helen that when he had been asked to go to the scene of the crime to identify his murdered son, he had knelt down by the body and had prayed the Lord's Prayer. When he got to the lines 'Forgive us our sins, as we forgive those who sin against us', he made himself pray those words and continued, 'Whoever did this, I forgive them.' But he said that he still found it difficult to overcome feelings of anger and bitterness when he remembered his son. Each birthday he felt as though he lost him over again. Forgiveness is never easy, he explained, every day he had to pray for it, struggle for it and win it.

What Do You Think?

1. Why did praying become important for Lloyd LeBlanc?

2. What do you think Lloyd LeBlanc meant when he said that every day he had to struggle for forgiveness? Is forgiveness always instantaneous or is there a process of forgiveness?

3. What evidence is there that Lloyd LeBlanc was really trying to forgive?

4. Can anyone ever really forget a traumatic experience? What do people mean when they encourage others to forgive and forget?

5. What might be the effect on someone's life if they cannot forgive?

A Nun in Hollywood

Helen tried not to grin with nervous excitement as she heard someone call out from the crowd of camera operators and producers in front of her, 'OK, get ready for the first take.' She still couldn't believe she was going to be in a Hollywood film. She smiled when she thought about all the children who dream of becoming film stars. She had never wanted to be a glamorous actress. How ironic that she, a middle-aged nun, was suddenly in the camera light and chatting comfortably with famous Hollywood stars.

As the lights glared around her, she tried to ignore the moving cameras and the huge microphones and concentrate on her 'acting'. She was in a crowd of people protesting about the death penalty outside the gates of a prison. Inside someone was about to be executed. She stood in a circle of people who were lighting candles and praying for the prisoner, the victims of the crime and the executioner. Next to her stood the actress Susan Sarandon, who was playing the lead role of 'Helen Prejean' in the film and who would go on to win an Oscar for her performance.

Several years after she had witnessed Sonnier's execution, Helen decided to write a book about her experiences. It was called *Dead Man Walking*. The book sold well and was awarded a literary prize. Tim Robins, a film director, had been inspired by it and now he was making it into a movie. Although Helen had only a small acting part, she also worked hard as a consultant, making all the scenes as true to life as possible. Her hope was that the film would be able to transport the audience straight to Angola Prison to see and hear the reality of Death Row.

The film was released in 1994 and was a box-office success. People from all over America and all over the world learnt what a difference Helen's faith in action had made. She became famous overnight. She was asked to take part in several chat shows and television documentaries, including the BBC *Everyman* programme.

As a result many people now support her and her hopes of abolishing the death penalty in the United States. However other people strongly disagree with her. Some have sent petitions against her to the Catholic Church. Sometimes she has been verbally abused. She feels as though she is never far from controversy. Her strong views and opinions have made her friends and enemies.

Despite her fame, Sister Helen Prejean continues to live in the St Thomas Housing Project. She splits her time between helping those living around her and campaigning for the abolition of the death penalty. She describes herself as 'an ordinary person involved in extraordinary events'.

What Do You Think?

1. Is Helen right to describe herself as an ordinary person? Give reasons.

2. How do you think Helen feels when she is criticized and verbally abused for campaigning against the death penalty and doing what she believes to be right? How do you cope when you are criticized? What pressures would stop you from doing something you believed to be right?

3. Why, after Helen had the excitement of being featured in a Hollywood movie and even acting in it, do you think she chose to carry on doing the same things and helping the same people?

4. Try to describe something so important to you that nothing would stop you pursuing it.

Biographical Notes

Helen Prejean was born in Baton Rouge, Louisiana in 1939. She joined the Sisters of St Joseph of Medaille in 1957. As a nun she worked hard, receiving a degree in English and Education in 1962 and a higher degree in Religious Education in 1973. Her work as a nun has included teaching high-school students.

She moved to the St Thomas Housing Project in New Orleans in 1981. Six months later she started to write to Elmo Patrick Sonnier, an inmate on Death Row in Angola Prison. On 15 September 1982 she visited Sonnier for the first time. She continued to visit him regularly. Sonnier was told he would be executed on 19 August 1983, but thirty-six hours before he was due to die he received a stay of execution. Sonnier was finally executed by electric chair on 4 April 1984. Helen Prejean was his spiritual adviser and was able to be with him during his final days, hours and execution itself. It was an experience she claimed changed her life.

Later she became a spiritual adviser for two other men and also witnessed their deaths. Since then she has devoted her energies to campaigning against the death penalty through lecturing and writing. She wrote a book about her experiences called *Dead Man Walking* which was turned into a major Hollywood film in 1994. Through the film Helen Prejean and her work and experiences became internationally known.

Things to Do

1 Imagine you belong to a group of people who plan to demonstrate outside a prison during an execution. You have been given the responsibility of designing the banner. Decide whether you are campaigning for or against the death penalty and make your banner.

2 Imagine you are producing a one-hour television documentary on Helen Prejean. Decide how you will divide the time, whom you would like to interview on the programme and where you would like to do some on-site filming. List your ideas together with the questions you would like to ask Helen Prejean herself.

3 Draw a map of the United States of America. Find out which states still use the death penalty and mark them on the map. Find out which other countries use the death penalty.

4 Imagine it is the week of an execution. Write a diary for this week as **one** of the following:

(a) A member of the family of a victim whose murderer is on Death Row
(b) A prison guard working on Death Row
(c) Someone who has a member of their family on Death Row

5 Organize a survey on people's responses to use of the death penalty. (Before you begin, write down what percentage of people you think will be for or against it.) Illustrate the results of your survey on a graph. Write a paragraph explaining your results and how they compare with your expectations.

6 Imagine a group of people move to a remote island to create a new community. Imagine you are on the island and you have been given responsibility for writing the rules. Write a maximum of ten rules, including a rule on murder, and decide what the punishment will be for each rule if it is broken.

7 If one of your friends or family had been murdered, what do you think your views on capital punishment would be? Spend a few minutes writing down your ideas then compare your ideas in small groups.

8 You are hoping to be the next American President. Write a short campaign speech clearly explaining your views on capital punishment. Would you want to increase or decrease the number of executions each year? Find out what the current President's position is on capital punishment and the opinions of his/her opponents.

9 Someone writes a letter to your local newspaper explaining why they support capital punishment. They write:

> Execution is an excellent deterrent. It is a specific deterrent, as there is no chance that the murderer could escape or be released from prison and commit another crime. It is also a general deterrent, as the execution of one person is a warning to others not to murder and could stop other similar crimes.

Think about this argument and write a letter to the paper in reply. You can agree or disagree but explain your reasons. Use no more than 200 words.

10 Does anyone have the right to take a life for a life? Organize a class debate on this question.

11 Write a poem to help and comfort someone who may be facing death. You may wish to use Psalm 31 to give you some ideas.

12 Imagine you have been asked to write an article for a national newspaper on your opinions on youth and crime. Explain at what age you think children know right from wrong, if you think children should be tried in a court in the same way as an adult, and if they should receive different punishments from adults.

13 Find references to forgiveness in the New Testament of the Bible. Put the verses into your own words.

Questions for Assessment or Examination Candidates

14 In the Christian Lord's Prayer, it says: 'Forgive us our sins, as we forgive those who sin against us.'

(a) Explain how a person opposed to the death penalty might use these words in support of their point of view. (10 marks)

(b) Suggest a biblical passage which would support the opposite point of view. (5 marks)

(c) 'Anyone who kills must be prepared to be killed.' Explain why you agree or disagree with this statement. (5 marks)

15 (a) Give **two** reasons for campaigning for the death penalty. (5 marks)

(b) Give **two** reasons for opposing the death penalty. (5 marks)

(c) 'In a civilized society, people should move away from the old idea of an eye for an eye.' How far do you agree or disagree with this statement? In your answer you must refer to the teaching of at least one religious tradition you have studied. (10 marks)

Religious and Moral Education Press
*A division of SCM-Canterbury Press Ltd,
a wholly owned subsidiary of
Hymns Ancient & Modern Ltd
St Mary's Works, St Mary's Plain
Norwich, Norfolk NR3 3BH*

First published 2000
Reprinted 2003

ISBN 1 85175 219 6

Designed and typeset by
TOPICS – The Creative Partnership,
Exeter

Cover illustration by Jane Taylor

Printed in Great Britain by
Brightsea Press, Exeter for
Religious and Moral Education Press,
Norwich

Notes for Teachers

The first Faith in Action books were published in the late 1970s and the series has remained popular with both teachers and pupils. However, much in education has changed over the last twenty years, such as the development of both new examination syllabuses in Religious Studies and local agreed syllabuses for Religious Education which place more emphasis on pupils' own understanding, interpretation and evaluation of religious belief and practice, rather than a simple knowledge of events. This has encouraged us to amend the style of the Faith in Action Series to make it more suitable for today's classroom.

The aim is, as before, to tell the stories of people who have lived and acted according to their faith, but we have included alongside the main story questions which will encourage pupils to think about the reasons for the behaviour of our main characters and to empathize with the situations in which they found themselves. We hope that pupils will also be able to relate some of the issues in the stories to other issues in modern society, either in their own area or on a global scale.

The 'What Do You Think?' questions may be used for group or class discussion or for short written exercises. The 'Things to Do' at the end of the story include ideas for longer activities and more-structured questions suitable for assessment or examination practice.

In line with current syllabus requirements, as Britain is a multifaith society, Faith in Action characters will be selected from a wide variety of faith backgrounds and many of the questions may be answered from the perspective of more than one faith.

CMB, 1997

Acknowledgements

The verses from the Bible on pages 8, 10 and 14 are quoted from the *Good News Bible* published by The Bible Societies/HarperCollins Publishers Ltd UK © American Bible Society, 1966, 1971, 1976, 1992.

The diary extract on page 5 is reproduced from *Dead Man Walking*, by Helen Prejean (HarperCollins, 1993). The conversation between Sonnier and Helen on page 13 is reproduced (slightly adapted) from the report of this exchange in *Dead Man Walking*. Elsewhere the story is based on descriptions of events in *Dead Man Walking* except on page 4, where the reaction of the families to the disappearance of the young people prior to the finding of the bodies is speculation. Illustrations of characters, apart from Helen, are not intended to be portraits of the real people involved.

This book has been published in association with The Stapleford Centre, The Old Lace Mill, Frederick Road, Stapleford, Nottingham NG9 8FN. Tel. 0115 939 6270. Website: www.stapleford-centre.org